I0166182

Joseph G. Jamison

Seven secrets in Husbandry

Joseph G. Jamison

Seven secrets in Husbandry

ISBN/EAN: 9783743344624

Manufactured in Europe, USA, Canada, Australia, Japa

Cover: Foto ©Lupo / pixelio.de

Manufactured and distributed by brebook publishing software
(www.brebook.com)

Joseph G. Jamison

Seven secrets in Husbandry

Seven Secrets

IN HUSBANDRY.

BEING THE

General Principles of Economical Life, with Instructions for Industrial Pursuits

BY

JOSEPH G. JAMISON,

KIRKSVILLE, MO.

Entered According to Act of Congress in
the year 1895, by
JOSEPH G. JAMISON,
in the office of the Librarian of Congress
at Washington.

CONTENTS.

INTRODUCTION.

....

THIS little volume has been prepared with the design of furnishing a deserving class of our people with information that is calculated to bring to them better returns for their labor. The different subjects have been commented upon to some extent, but the matter in each division has been reduced to as small space as circumstances would admit of. The contents of this volume is of an expensive character; it has been hard to get and has cost a great deal of both time and money, but the author has for several years been of the belief that it is better to buy the experi- of others than to use up the most useful part of our own lives trying experiments. As small as this work is, the reader will find it to contain more real value than has heretofore been published in large and expensive volumes. The author feels confident that all who may read this book will be well satisfied with their venture and be proud of a courage that has induced them to try to gather information on these subjects.

How to Destroy Insects About the Orchard and Garden.

EVERY ONE who has lived fifty years knows that insects did not interfere with fruit in the newly settled parts of this country. But at this time apples, as hardy a thing as they are, are apparantly eaten up by the worms. I will ask, why is this? When the reader's mind is called to the fact they will see the trouble at once. Fifty years back there was a very large scope of country that had no settlements, and many parts were thinly settled, and all sorts of fruit were grown with very little care. The birds were as thick as the cattle-fly in latter days; as the country settled up and the timber was destroyed the birds had to fall back, or, I will say, they had to go with the Indians, and have been treated much like the buffalo of our plains. This government has imported birds to some extent, but there is no use in trying to maintain a variety of birds in this country for many years to come. The people are too destructive and the towns are too

thick to accomplish anything in that way.
Every family can maintain a flock of birds of
their own large enough to use up all the insects about the place, and they will never
trouble anything but insects and work only
for the family that prepares nests for them.
That bird is the little house wren. It is said
that one pair of them will catch and carry to
their young in one day's time eight or ten
hundred insects. The wren is a very prolific
bird; they raise from two to three broods of
young each year, and no one would think of
injuring a wren; the cat is the only enemy
they have and the wren will beat the cat every time if you will put their next-boxes up
right. Make boxes about four by six inches,
with a hole in them about an inch in size,
nail them up on the sides and ends of your
out-buildings, or where the wrens can find
them, and your part of the work is done.

How to Put Out Fruit Trees That Will Last More Than One Generation.

THE growing of fruit has become a critical business, and the Amerinan people are very much discouraged as to the probable outcome. The deterioration of our orchards has been increasing for several years. Farmers who were a few years ago relying upon their orchards for ready money, now have in some instances, to buy fruit or have their families deprived of its use. The thinking people are now looking the grounds over to see if they can discover the reason for this change. Our investigations have caused us to believe that all of this loss of trees and their fruit has been brought about mostly by our own hands. While we may be told that the decaying vegetation is of a different character now to what it was in an early day, it is equally proper for us to say if the timber had been left standing, the results in that particular would be about the same. The reader must admit that the destruction of the timber and of our birds would naturally bring about a change of some sort. We think deception has also figured to some extent in this matter; and to be more pointed, we will say that the dealers in trees have done their part in bringing about this destruction of fruit trees. The nursery business never would have been worth anything if the fruit business had been conducted in a natural way, and the reader will bear in mind that when nature is interferred with it always makes trouble. Dealers in fruit trees found it to their interest to make, to a certain extent, false statements in regard to the production of fruit. To begin with, the farmer could grow trees from the seed as well as any dealer in trees could, which is the key to the whole matter. And there could be no reliable dealers in trees if produced in that way: they could not know what sort of fruit their trees might produce, and it has been to their advantage to tell the people that fruit from the seed was not so good as grafted trees would produce; in fact, they could point out trees of a worthless character and at the same time exhibit specimens of unusually good fruit from grafts. This fine appearing fruit being flaunted before the eyes of purchasers, they

naturally would forget how good fruit originates, and while the dealer must admit that
all fruits came from the seed, they always
made it a point to inform purchasers that
such a production as their fruit could hardly
be produced in a lifetime from seed. To produce trees that will last one's lifetime, they
must be produced from the seed, and it is all
a mistake that good fruit cannot be produced
in that way. We very readily admit that a
great deal of poor fruit may come from the
seed, but it is easy to arrange for such a
thing. Every one should know that good
apples do not grow on thorn trees. We must
plant seed from the sort of fruit that we want
to grow, and we have about as many chances
to get better fruit as to get worse—that is
Nature's rule in all things. The proper way
to grow trees is to plant seed from good specimens, in good soil, in rows about four feet
apart, and after they start to grow well, thin
them to from ten to fifteen inches apart, and
cultivate well, then the second or third year
go through and thin out again, taking out
all the dwarfs and rough-looking trees, sav-
ing all that are smooth and vigorous in appearance. One with a good eye can pick a

good tree from the appearance of its leaves and the manner in which its branches appear; in fact, one can pick a young tree that will produce the same fruit that the parent tree did; if any of them show some remarkable points they should always be retained and the bad-looking ones destroyed. In this way you will get into your orchard very little poor fruit. The small trees should be set where the orchard is to stand, and cultivate them well as long as the branches of the trees will admit of it, and if it is necessary to set the trees on ground that cannot be cultivated, we should dig about the trees and mulch well with straw or coarse weeds, but in either case to keep away the worms we should have a flock of our house wrens, and a stock of liquid manure which we prepare by locating a barrel or hogshead and filling it one-third full of unleached horse manure and filling up with water. Let it stand six or eight days, keeping it stirred up well; then apply about one gallon of the strong liquid to the trunks and roots of each tree twice a week after sunset through the spring and up to the middle of the summer, putting in fresh manure as the liquid becomes diluted. This will keep

the worms out and invigorate the trees. We
want to grow the trees without their receiv-
ing any blemishes to cause decay. If we suc-
ceed in this we have trees, if grown from the
seed, that will last more than one generation.

How to Produce a Milk and Butter Herd of Cattle.

EVFRY ONE who has handled milch cows
knows that there is a wonderful difference in their production of milk and butter.
and it is rather well understood that for
milking purposes it is better to save heifers
from good milking cows. We will admit this
to be the better course, but at the same time
we will find but a small per cent. of heifers
picked up in this way that will meet our ex-
pectations. To produce a milking herd of
cattle, we must start right. We must have a
cow that is a good milk and butter producer,
and is capable of conveying her qualities to
her offspring. There are but few cows of this
sort, but they can be found in almost any
neighborhood, and their owners know or
care but little for these qualities, while at the

same time they are possessed of a cow of the most valuable type; for once possessed of a cow of this sort, we are fixed for life. We do not have to fool away the most useful part of our lives changing cows. How this peculiar habit originates is hard to tell, but we have learned enough from the human race to know that it first originates through the female, and if it is well fixed it will never run out, no matter what they are bred to. There are different degrees of power in conveying this habit, and if your cow is a little weak but sure in this matter, we must mate her with a male out of a cow of this sort—that would be the proper course with any cow. The female that impresses a habit like this is about as likely to make the impression in a bull as a heifer calf. The origin of this peculiar habit is something like a strawberry on the child's head—it is as apt to be on a male as a female, and the child is always ready to eat strawberries, and the mother can tell you why it is so, though the cow cannot tell you about her calf. Some have it that this milking habit started through the male, as they sometimes transfer it regularly, but it is forgotten what he may have had for a dam.

How to Prevent Abortion in Animals.

ABORTION often assumes an epidemic character affecting whole herds, and at times will include a large extent of country. We are told that to prevent abortion or to stop its progress, we must ascertain the cause or causes producing it, but this has been a difficult point for the profession to determine. While professional writers mention many causes which are supposed to produce common or sporadic abortion, we are inclined to think the main cause has been overlooked. Abortion that assumes an epidemic character can almost always be traced to herds which have been well housed and fed concentrated food. We seldom find abortion prevailing to any great extent where cattle sleep and eat in the open air. While stables seem to be almost indispensable to dairymen they should prepare themselves to prevent abortions in their herds by having perfect ventilation, and the next thing should be to prepare a variety of food, for there is no question but that confinement in a foul atmosphere and being highly fed on a single concentrated food will in itself produce abortion. We think stock of any sort to do well and keep healthy should have a change of food, and if stockmen will feed one-half pint of hemp seed to their cows every fourth or fifth day through the winter or during pregnancy, there will be no abortions in that herd. This remedy has been used to some extent for many years, but not always to an advantage on account of the manner in which it has been administered. Parties who have recommended hemp seed in abortions have always left the impression that there was time enough to doctor after the cows get sick. We think the proper course would be to feed the seed before they get sick so that they may remain healthy.

How to Remove the Afterbirth.

COWS in producing calves, are at times unable to expel the placenta, or after birth. When the afterbirth is retained any length of time the cow becomes feverish and very feeble. In such cases families have been deprived of the cow's milk for months. This can all be avoided by removing the afterbirth which should be done within twenty-four hours after parturition. Veterinarians advise the introduction of the hand to loosen the confined parts. This, however, requires some experience to be successful in the operation. Retention of the afterbirth seems to be brought about by contraction of the neck of the womb soon after parturition. The placenta containing a row of large lumps, it is impossible for the cow to expel the substance after the parts contract behind them. If we cause the neck of the womb to dilate, the cow has but little trouble in discharging the substance. We have been successful in bringing this about with the use of flax seed. As soon as we find that the afterbirth is being retained, we mix between one and two ounces of whole flax seed with the cow's oats or bran twice a day until she gets relief. Whole flax seed, when administered in reasonable quantities, will always dilate the neck of the womb sufficiently to pass the placenta, which is done through a natural effort of the cow. After this takes place there is nothing to be done more than to nurse the cow for a few days until she regains her strength. Oil-cakes made from flax seed do not have the desired effect; it seems that extracting the oil from flax seed destroys this peculiar effect.

Why a Few Parties Breed Better Animals Than Others.

THE breeding of good animals is always the result of knowledge or a mere accident. The production of live stock has now too much expense attached to it to rely upon accidental breeding. There have always been a few men in this country who knew what was required to produce a good animal, but they have, when speaking of their peculiar way of breeding, misled their hearers. If we expect to produce good animals, we must mate good things together, and to do this we must be prepared to know good things when we see them. To grow a first-class animal it has got to be able to digest all the food that its stomach will hold, and that sort of an animal has its peculiar make-up, and its muscular formation indicates the amount of power it may have in that particular. We will select cattle as a subject in this article. It has been said that it is useless to try to breed away the faults of an old cow; if that be true, it would be equally hard to breed away her good points, and her good or bad feeding qualities are brought about by the strength of her muscles. We can see the size and elasticity of the muscles at the points where they come together, and the most noted points of meeting are the navel and rectum. It can be seen better in the calf—a calf with a large and firm navel and a rectum with such large and strong muscles that ridges are formed about its terminus. We would expect a calf of that sort to feed and grow well—makes of this sort indicate endurance. This sort of a cow will stand shipping to market with half the loss or shrinkage that the average cow will. These marks in a breeding bull indicate a sure and a regular breeder; his calves will feed well and seldom scour or founder. It seems to be natural for cattle to throw off excrement in case of excitement or placed in a strange position, and those that have flabby muscles have no power to control themselves in this respect which 'always terminates in a loss of flesh. We get the idea in using horses. We bring out a horse for a few hours' drive; he appears to be healthy and in a fine fix; as soon as he is put in motion we get the result of his muscular power;

if his rectum, or anus is large and flabby he will throw off a large amount of excrement and in a few hours he will begin to fag and will very soon appear like a horse that had been badly treated. On the other hand if our horse has his muscles well concentrated and strong at the points before mentioned, his appearance after being used will be entirely different from the first horse described.

How to Grow Calves That do not Scour.

MOST every cattle man has more or less trouble with his calves' digestive organs. It is very annoying for our calves to be always running off at the bowels. There are two reasons for this trouble—one is a scrofulous nature that has been inherited, but the most prevailing cause originates in the dam's milk. It is not known by every one that the most effective way to administer medicine to a suckling of any sort is to put it in the dam's feed. We knew a very intelligent man a few years ago to kill a whole litter of pigs by giving the mother medicine. It never hurt the mother for the reason that she was much older than the pigs. If a calf has no scrofula it is not so hard to keep it healthy and thriving, and it is much better to guard the mother than the calf. We want to feed the cow food that is easily digested. If she be fed grain, it should be in small quantities, and mill-feed seems to have a worse effect on the calf than corn; it seems as if Nature had formed the cow's stomach for the consumption of grass. In herds of pedigreed stock we often find cattle that have had their stomachs so impaired when small that they could barely take food enough to keep them alive. Think of stuffing the tender stomach of a new born calf with corn or any other concentrated food. Bear in mind that what we feed the cow the calf gets if it takes her milk. Give the calf time for its stomach to prepare for these things and then they will not set up inflammation in the lining membranes of the stomach and intestines. If it is necessary to feed the cow to produce milk and butter, and the calf is inclined to scour bad, you may add to the mother's feed one tablespoonful of powdered chalk twice a day, which will hold it in check.

How to Fight the Cattle-Fly.

THE little cattle-fly has become so bold within the last few years that the people feel worried with them. Inquiries have been sent out asking for relief if it could be had. State experiment stations have taken the matter into consideration and so far have only found temporary relief from any substance they have tried. Parties have been advertising remedies as a sure and permanent thing to keep off the fly. We find their remedy to be tar and oil made firm with a harder substance, and it is very unhandy to apply, and but few persons ever apply it more than once. Tar in any form will frighten the fly away for a while, but as soon as they learn that it will not stick them fast they return to their work. Grease of any sort is disliked by these pests; they know that they cannot wade through it if it is very deep. After all the information we can get and the experience we have, we think the best and most convenient course for owners of stock would be to prepare a mixture of tar and oil. You can use any cheap oil that flows well, such as cotton seed or fish oil, and to make it more convenient we would use one ounce of the oil of tar to two ounces of fish oil. Prepare a woolen cloth filled with the mixture and rub down the horse or cow about three times a week. The mixture will dampen the hair and make the animal look sleek if rubbed properly. Horses should be rubbed with the mixture every time they are taken out; if this is done our horse does not only look well, but will remain more quiet for the reason that he is not being troubled with the flies.

How to Destroy Moles or Gophers.

THE ground mole costs the people a great deal of trouble as well as some loss of crops. There has been a general inquiry as to what could be done to destroy them. Two or three moles will work over a good-sized garden. The people have tried poisoning them without much success. Bisulphide of carbon is a simple agent for the destruction of moles. It is used by saturating a bunch of cotton or rags with it and introducing it into their runs by opening a place that has recently been worked up; place the saturated package well into the run and then close up the opening good so that the gas may not escape. Bisulphide of carbon is often hard to get and is an inflamable substance, which makes against its use. We can destroy the mole or gopher with sulphur, a remedy kept about almost every house. In using sulphur for this work you take some small tin cake-pans of the toy sort, open a place in a freshly worked run, removing the dirt carefully, and cut out a place in the bottom of the run that will fit your vessel; fill the vessel with fire-coals, put on the sulphur, cover up the open-ing with a board and cover the board with the loose dirt to confine the smoke from the sulphur; and a better and a surer way is to have a small hand-bellows, such as have been kept for fire starters, insert the point of this bellows through the dirt near the fire, and blow the gases down the run and it will keep the fire burning as well. Do this as often as you find freshly made runs and your moles will disappear.

How to Keep Eggs Fresh From One Year to Another.

THE loss of the summer laid eggs is a drawback to the poultry business. While the cold storage system is of some value, eggs have often deteriorated before they reach the storage-room. To put eggs away fresh in hot weather, we should be prepared to pack them each day, for they should have no time to shrink before they are put away. To make the packing satisfactory you should prepare a suitable vessel—an empty nail keg will do for eight or ten dozen. Place your vessel in a cool and dry place; put in the bottom of the vessel about two inches of wheat bran or mixed mill-stuff, get a woolen rag and a little hog's lard, grease the rag and rub the grease all over the eggs and place them on end in the bran, something near an inch apart and from the sides of the vessel; when a layer of them are in, ffll up with bran, making a thickness above the eggs of about two inches, then put down in the same way until the vessel is full, leaving the top for a covering two inches thick. Let them stand until they are wanted for use or market. When we want an egg for use we take it out without any need for disarranging the remaining ones. When we want to remove the eggs from the bran we have a cloth and rub them over as they are lifted out. With this process eggs will keep for months if they are put in fresh and sound; the slightest crack in the shell will spoil them, and a rough or thin shelled egg should never be put away.

How to Keep Butter Fresh.

THE making and keeping of butter in good condition any length of time is of some importance to nearly every family. For butter to become firm and sweet the milk should be well worked out of it before any attempt is made to pack it away. To keep butter in a small way we get a stone jar and its size may be regulated by the amount of butter that we want to put in it. Place the jar in a box, keg or barrel, as it may be, large enough to pack a layer of salt two inches thick all around the jar; put two inches of salt in the box to set the jar on, then pack all around tight with salt up to the top of the jar, having first placed them in a dry and cool place where they should remain permanently. If the butter is firm enough to form rolls, we can put them away one roll at a time if we choose to do so. We first put a thin layer of salt in the bottom of the jar; then prepare a cloth of suitable size, saturate it well with sweet lard and roll up the butter in the cloth, covering the butter all over with the cloth, put it in the jar so that it will not touch the sides, and pack them in the same way, side by side, filling in between them with salt and level up each time with salt for a new layer of butter, and when the jar is within about four inches of the top, fill out with salt and cover over the top with a board, or a greased cloth would be better. When you want to use butter lift out one roll at a time and turn back the cloth far enough to cut off what you want and then roll up again. Your butter will be good for all time if good when put down. If your butter be too soft to roll, you then grease the inside of the jar with lard and pack in the butter tight, putting a greased cloth between each batch, and when you are near the top, put over the greased cloth and on top of that put lard about one inch thick. This will keep good but is not so convenient for use. Butter can be hardened hard enough to roll by hanging a while in a deep well or set in cold water for a short time.

How to Advance Melons Ten Days.

IN many parts of several of the states the difference of ten days time in producing melons would be a profitable item in that business. In a clay soil vines of every sort start to grow very slowly in the early spring, and about the time they get to growing well the hot and dry season is at hand and it dwarfs their fruit. It has been a common practice to force the growth of vines with stale manure. While this creates some warmth and starts the vines to grow vigorously they cannot stand the dry part of the season as well as if they never had any manure. The most effective way to start vines to grow early in the spring and to keep them growing well is to use the liquid manure made from unleached horse manure—prepared as directed in our second chapter. When we want to plant melon seed we dig a small hole where we want to make the hill, and fill the hole with this strong liquid; we draw in soil and have it get thoroughly wet with the liquid, as soon as the liquid has disappeared we plant the seed in the wet dirt and cover the wet space with dry dirt. Cultivate well while starting to vine and use the plow as much as possible. Insects will be inclined to pass your vines until hot weather, when we spray the vines with the liquid once or twice a week —always after sundown. The liquid will keep away the striped bug which is so destructive in hot weather. After a few melons have set on the vines we pinch off the ends of the vines, but pinch none that have no melons set on. Vines of any sort do better when they have something to hold to; if it was not to their advantage to hold to something they would not have holders on their vines; if there is something for their holders to catch to the fruit will be larger and mature better.

How to Advance Strawberries Seven Days.

STRAWBERRIES are one of the most profitable small crops that a farmer can grow. Some have argued that they require too much attention, which is quite a mistake. While it is true that strawberries are some trouble to plant out, but after that the work is not so hard, nor do we find them so troublesome. They should be planted reasonably close so that they will run together the first year. The second year, after the crop has been gathered, we would plow under a strip about five or six feet wide and leave from five to six feet and plow another strip until the patch has been gone over, and then harrow the plowed part well with a fine-toothed harrow. The patch should be rather long to be convenient to work. The next year plow up the old strips and work it in the same way. The worked strips will fill up with vines each fall so that there is no more setting of plants, and the grass will not take the bed and the berries are larger. In growing strawberries the season can be extended much longer by planting early, medium and late varieties, and it is useless to plant anything that is not reasonably hardy and good producers; in this way, with very slight protection through the winter, a strawberry bed will stand for years. To bring on the berries early and to enlarge the fruit, use freely the liquid manure prepared as directed in the second chapter. Always apply the liquid after sunset. The liquid should be sprinkled or sprayed on the plants. Nothing will pay better than the use of this liquid on strawberries. It does not seed the bed and it invigorates the plants and brightens the fruit, and as a rule it will tide the vines over a very dry spell; it fills out all the fruit instead of drying it up on the stems.

How to Keep the Peach Trees Bearing

WHEN we think the matter over it seems so strange that so large a per cent. of people would give up the culture of so valuable a fruit as peaches. One would think, under such circumstances, more people would make them a specialty. It seems that the winter-killing and the worms have discouraged the lovers of this fruit over a large scope of our country. Where peach trees have been winter-killed, they nearly always sprout up from the stump anew; if one will cut the old tree away and thin out the sprouts to about three good ones and have them as far apart as you can, and when the sap is right bud or graft the sprouts with such fruit as you like, and you can put in different sorts of fruit so that apparently the same tree is ripening fruit all the season. To keep the sprouts healthy and their fruit sound, you should use the liquid manure prepared as directed in our second chapter. Pour about one gallon of liquid around the roots of the trees every one or two weeks, and while in bloom spray the

trees with the strong liquid. As soon as the
weeds get large enough, cut them and put
them about the trunks of the trees when the
ground is not being cultivated. It is a good
thing to let a new sprout grow every two or
three years; in this way you are sure not to
have them all winter-kill; however, the worms
do the trees more harm than the winters, and
this liquid and our little birds described in
another part of this book, will finish the
worms and leave your trees to furnish a valuable lot of fruit.

How to Profit by a Variation in Animal Reproduction.

THE matter of variations in reproducing animals have been written upon by many writers, and some of them have undertaken to give some probable cause for such a difference in animals reproducing themselves, but such things can only be an imagination; and it seems as far as history knows that there never was any species of animal that has not had some radical variations. The American deer has often been referred to as one of the animals that breed true to color, and at the shme time white deer have been seen at different times. Some writers speak of it as something that cannot be accounted for, but we think it can easily be accounted for when we admit that these things have to be so. If the deer at times must change its color, what could we expect but a change to white rather than any other color, for when we look the animal over we find about one-third of the hair that makes up its coat white. It seems that nature has provided a law that governs the reproduction of both vegetable and animal life. If animals did not vary in reproducing themselves they would all be alike; you could not tell one from another, which would make the world monotonous. These variations have been found to run about equal for better and worse, larger and smaller, and it runs all the way through in that way. It seems that this is nature's way of holding animal life about the same without having it look alike. One would think if this is all true that breeders of live stock could profit but very little by these variations. The point in this matter is that while breeding we adopt some of these peculiarities to our own idea or to the demands of the country, which breeders sometimes call forming a new breed. If we want to increase the size of our horses, the better way is to select our breeding stock from mares that we have known and know their offspring. If a mare should have a colt from the same horse that is much larger than the other ones, and not bad other ways, that is the animal we want to breed from to increase size, for it will always produce larger stock than its family has been, and if you can mate it with another that got its size in the same way, we get the thing fixed so that it will last for all time, In this way we can fix any of these peculiarities that we wish to adopt so that they will stay and be reproduced for many years. This idea nearly always calls for inbreeding to some extent, and at times the first one or two crosses are so pleasing that the breeder gets excited and continues it until he spoils the whole thing. Inbreeding will fix a type in animals, but type fixed in that way is not worth near so much as one created by mateing two sports in a similar variation from two original types.

www.ingramcontent.com/pod-product-compliance
Lightning Source LLC
Chambersburg PA
CBHW032142080426
42733CB00008B/1168